Rookie Poetry™
Animal Homes

# my home on the ice

J. Patrick Lewis

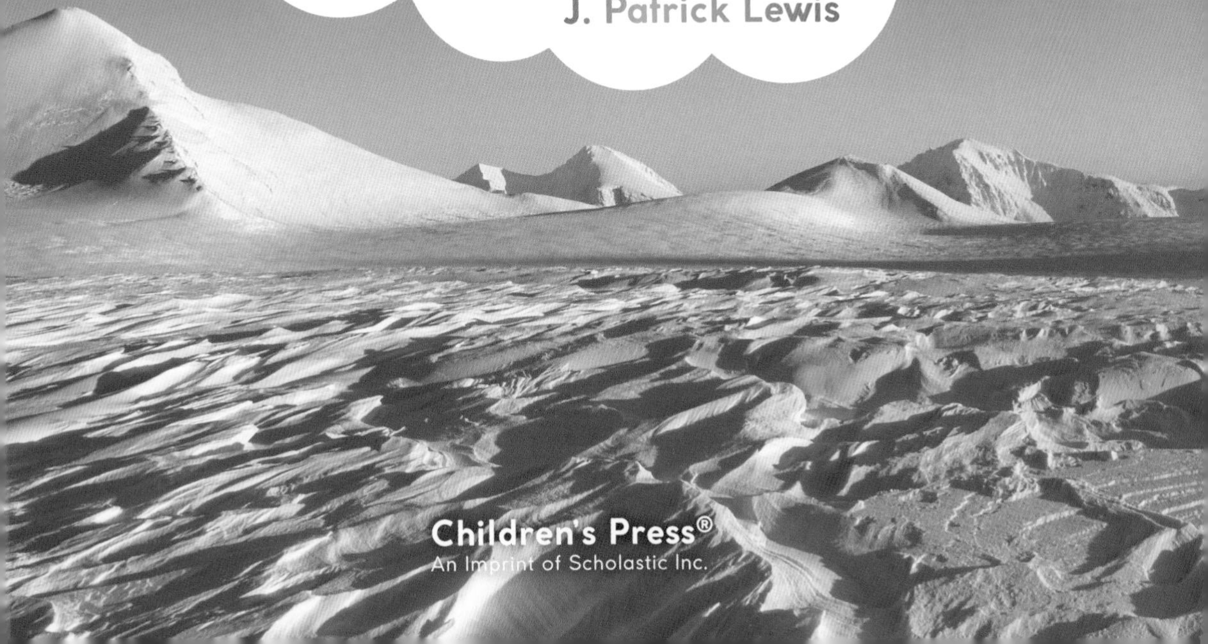

Children's Press®
An Imprint of Scholastic Inc.

Library of Congress Cataloging-in-Publication Data
Names: Lewis, J. Patrick, author.
Title: My home on the ice/by J. Patrick Lewis.
Description: New York, NY : Children's Press, an Imprint of Scholastic Inc., 2017.
| Series: Rookie poetry. Animal homes | Includes index.
Identifiers: LCCN 2016030839| ISBN 9780531228722 (library binding) | ISBN 9780531230077 (pbk.)
Subjects: LCSH: Ecology—Arctic regions—Juvenile literature.
Classification: LCC QH84.1 .L49 2017 | DDC 577.0911/3—dc23
LC record available at https://lccn.loc.gov/2016030839



Produced by Spooky Cheetah Press
Design by Anna Tunick


Printed in China 62



2 3 4 5 6 7 8 9 10 R 26 25 24 23 22 21 20 19 18 17

Photos ©: cover: Design Pics Inc/Alamy Images; back cover background: Erectus/Dreamstime; back cover penguin: Martin Ruegner/Getty Images; back cover bird: David Wall Photo/Getty Images; back cover fox: Mark Sisson/Getty Images; cloud vector throughout: Freepik.com; 1: Erectus/Dreamstime; 2-3: Martin Harvey/Getty Images; 5: Staphy/Dreamstime; 7 background: Tui De Roy/Minden Pictures; 7 penguins: Martin Ruegner/Getty Images; 9: Jan Martin Will/Dreamstime; 11: Norbert Wu/Minden Pictures; 13 right ice clump: Colin Monteath/Hedgehog House/Minden Pictures; 13 main: Mark Sisson/Getty Images; 13 background: Erectus/Dreamstime; 15: Auscape/Getty Images; 17 background sky: Anna Tunick; 17 background iceberg: Bernard Breton/Dreamstime; 17 main: David Wall Photo/Getty Images; 19 background: Steve Allen/Dreamstime; 19 seal: Tui De Roy/Minden Pictures/Getty Images; 19 polar bear: Outdoorsman/Dreamstime; 19 bird: David Wall Photo/Getty Images; 19 fox: Mark Sisson/Getty Images; 19 penguin: Martin Ruegner/Getty Images; 20 left iceberg: Achim Baqué/Dreamstime; 20 right icebergs: Peter Sobolev/Dreamstime; 20 penguin: Martin Ruegner/Getty Images; 20 polar bear: Outdoorsman/Dreamstime; 20 seal: Tui De Roy/Minden Pictures/Getty Images; 20 center iceberg: Steve Allen/Dreamstime; 21 albatross: Winfred Wisniewski/Getty Images; 21 icebergs: Peter Sobolev/Dreamstime; 21 fox: Mark Sisson/Getty Images; 21 krill: Auscape/Getty Images; 23 top: Chase Dekker/Dreamstime; 23 center bottom: Neurobite/Dreamstime; 23 bottom: David Wall Photo/Getty Images; 23 center top: Tui De Roy/Minden Pictures/Getty Images.

Scholastic Inc.,557 Broadway,New York, NY 10012.

# table of contents

# Welcome to the ice

Who could survive in a frozen world?
Who would live in a kingdom of cold?
Mostly fast creatures with fur or with fat—
and only the clever, the brave, and the bold

The northern and southern extremes of Earth are covered in ice. They are called the poles.

# emperor penguin

This birdie was missing a part—
doctors noticed no knees on her chart.
But she knows how to flap with a **flipper**.
A butler with wings—pretty smart!

Emperor penguins sleep standing up rather than lying on the icy cold ground.

# polar bear

I am the king of the icebergs,
standing tall in my white fur coat,
alone on the melting **sea ice**,
trying to stay afloat.

A polar bear can smell prey from up to 20 miles away.

# weddell seal

I never leave my ice cap home.
I can dive 2,000 feet and remain
underwater for nearly an hour.
What a pleasingly freezing **domain**!

Weddell seals must poke their heads above water to breathe. In winter, they use their teeth to chew breathing holes in the ice.

# arctic fox

His jacket is snow white in winter;
in summer, he changes his clothes
to brown so he lives undercover
wherever an arctic fox goes.

An arctic fox
wraps itself in its
bushy tail to keep warm
in cold weather.

# antarctic krill

Life's quite a thrill for us half-inch krill (meaning "small fry of fishes"); we swim as fast as we can to escape from a whale so we don't become lunch for him!

Krill are the main prey of hundreds of animals, from fish to birds to whales!

# snowy albatross

I have the largest **wingspan**
of any living thing,
and I can fly for the next few hours
without ever flapping a wing.

Albatrosses, like other seabirds, drink salt water from the sea.

# icy homes

If you love a wintry wonderland that's frozen almost the whole year, then pack up your parkas and mittens and huskies, and join the reindeer.

The animals shown in this book are hiding in this photo. Can you find them all?

# fact files

| | Emperor Penguin | Polar Bear | Weddell Seal |
|---|---|---|---|
| HOW BIG AM I? | up to 45 inches tall *(about as tall as a six-year-old)* | up to 10 feet tall on hind legs *(same as a basketball hoop)* | up to 10 feet long *(more than twice as long as a bicycle)* |
| HOW MUCH DO I WEIGH? | up to 88 pounds *(about as much as a fifth grader)* | up to 1,600 pounds *(as much as three motorcycles)* | up to 1,200 pounds *(about 12 seventh graders)* |
| WHAT DO I EAT? | fish, squid, krill | seals | fish, crustaceans, octopuses |

| Arctic Fox | Antarctic Krill | Snowy Albatross |
|---|---|---|
| up to 30 inches long, including its tail *(almost as long as a yardstick)* | 2.4 inches long *(about as long as a toothpick)* | Wingspan: up to 11 feet across *(as long as two snowboards)* |
| up to 17 pounds *(about the same as two gallons of water)* | 0.035 ounces *(less than half a penny)* | up to 22 pounds *(about the same as a car tire)* |
| lemmings, birds, eggs, fish | tiny plants called phytoplankton | squid, fish |

# ice...the freezing facts

1. **The area of Earth covered by ice is called the arctic tundra.** It is one of the coldest places on Earth. Temperatures can go as low as -70° Fahrenheit (-57° Celsius). That is a lot colder than your freezer, which is 0° Fahrenheit!

2. **During the winter months, it is dark 24 hours a day.** In the summer, the sun never sets!

3. **Because icy regions are so cold, only a few animals can live there.**

4. **In icy regions, there is a layer right below the topsoil called permafrost.** Permafrost is always frozen. These are the only areas where entire bodies of extinct animals, like woolly mammoths, have been found.

5. **During the few months of summer, the tundra looks very different!** The ground is covered with colorful wildflowers that grow in the top layer of soil.

# glossary

**domain** (doh-MAYN): A region or place controlled by a government or person.

**flipper** (FLIP-uhr): One of the broad, flat limbs that sea mammals such as seals, whales, and dolphins use when they swim.

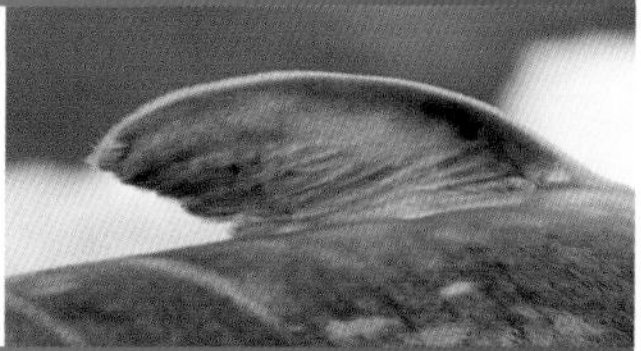

**sea ice** (SEE ISE): Masses of ice floating in the sea.

**wingspan** (WING-span): The distance from the tip of one wing of a bird to the tip of the other wing.

# index



# facts for now

Visit this Scholastic Web site to learn more about ice habitats and download the Teaching Guide for this series: **www.factsfornow.scholastic.com**
Enter the keyword **Ice**

# about the author

**J. Patrick Lewis** has published 100 children's picture and poetry books to date, with a wide variety of publishers. The Poetry Foundation named him the third U.S. Children's Poet Laureate.